WEALTH CREATION

THE INFLUENCER

The Influencer is a person WHO inspires or guides the actions of others.

Rob Wilson

(Wealth Creation - The Influencer)

ISBN 978-0-9721065-4-2

Printed in USA

Dedication

These series of Wealth Creation is dedicated to the many families that I have comes across in my work. It is also dedicated to you the now reader, whether you are reading just this book or the entire series, I am in prayer that you experience wealth creation personally.

I especially wish that you who have chosen to read this series find what they are seeking.

Rob Wilson

W

H

O

?

Sometimes it is your who that matters. Sometimes you have to know who it is. Sometimes you are guided by your who.

Knowing Your Who…

Table of Contents

Foreword I

Preface III

Introduction V

Chapter 1 – Insanity 1

Chapter 2 – Self Determine 9

Chapter 3 – Programming 15

Chapter 4 – Control 23

Chapter 5 – Behavior 33

Chapter 6 – The Circle Of 45

Chapter 7 – Friends or Family 53

Chapter 8 – Money 63

Chapter 9 – Next Generation 73

Chapter 10 – Building Your Legacy 81

Chapter 11 – My Final Words 93

Foreword

For years I have been a student of the great author, speaker, and leadership guru, Dr. John C. Maxwell. A foundational theme in Dr. Maxwell's work is the concept that "leadership is influence… nothing more, nothing less!" I couldn't be prouder of my friend and brother, Rob Wilson, who has decided to tackle the concept of "The Influencer" in his Wealth Creation series.

An "influencer" himself, Rob is the perfect person to apply such a concept to the wisdom of this series, as the old adage exclaims, "it takes one, to know one."

Rob has seen people with a platform and prominence come and go throughout his career. From politicians, to preachers, to prognosticators, to protagonists, many proclaim to have the answer to happiness and fulfillment. Some rest in the Old Testament proclamation, "…money answereth all things" (Ecc. 10:19) and search for it underneath every stray rock.

Others rely solely on declaration with, "name it and claim it" as their motto. Still others apply good old fashioned hard work to the engagement of their time and think that is enough. "Wealth Creation: The Influencer" does not discount any of these ideas.

It does, however, challenge you to consider the source of the idea even as you examine the person you are becoming. Who is the influencer? What influences your thinking in the process of creating wealth? How are you being transformed for sustainable wealth?

There is more to wealth creation than meets the eye. As a practitioner, mentor, public communicator, and generational thought leader, Rob has identified a formula that speaks right to the heart of wealth creation. Are you an influencer – a leader, change agent, trend setter?

Or are you the influenced? There is a place for both, but lasting wealth comes through application of truth. Allow Rob's words herein to guide your thinking about wealth creation, as you become a discerner of the times, who like the sons of Issachar, know what to do (1 Chronicles 12:32).

Dr. Christopher L. Boyd
Pastor, Word of Faith Family Worship Cathedral

Preface

The Way You Think and Feel.

Now it's time to uncovering how wealth creation impacts our sense of morality, our relationships with others, and our mental health. Yes, just like in my book "The Mindset" I tried to show the connection of wealth creation impacting all of us in many ways. It's an Influencer.

The term "affluenza"—a combination of affluence and influenza, defined as a "painful, contagious, socially transmitted condition of overload, debt, anxiety, and waste, resulting from the dogged pursuit of more"—is often dismissed as a silly buzzword created to express our cultural disdain for consumerism. Though often used in jest, the term may contain more truth than many of us would like to think.

The fact is affluenza real or imagined, money really does change everything, as the song goes—and those of wealth do tend to see themselves much differently than others. Wealth creation (and the pursuit of it) has been linked with moral and immoral behavior.

There is an impact of wealth and inequality on our behavior. Money can powerfully influence our thoughts and actions in ways that we're often not aware of, no matter our financial circumstances. We can be living paycheck to paycheck go about our daily lives as we have it all.

Although wealth creation or wealth it's self is certainly subjective, it's often measured on scales of income, job status, or socioeconomic circumstances, like educational attainment and intergenerational wealth and have shown that wealth may be at odds with empathy and compassion.

Wow, I wish you could feel the butterflies I am having right now. When it hits you I hope that you will enjoy the wisdom of know the money and wealth are different thing and impact differently. Lower income families are better at reading others' people than wealthier people.

Can money be an influencer?

This can sound like an inequality more than influencer, but I think it is important to set the right tone as we discuss money and wealth, the poor and the wealthy, the lower and the upper classes as it relates to finance.

A lot of times what often we see is a baseline for the lower class to be more empathetic and the upper class to be less. Lower-class individuals have to respond chronically to a number of vulnerabilities and financial threats.

They really need to depend on others so they will tell you if a social threat or opportunity is coming, and that makes you more perceptive of emotions. While a lack of resources fosters greater emotional intelligence, having more resources can cause bad behavior in its own right.

Introduction

Not long ago, people went about their lives not being defined by very much. What I mean about that statement is people rarely associated their lifestyle choices as a culture. Nor did they have vision or insight on wealth creation as a part of the fabric of their lives.

Wealth Creation and power are two things most people aspire to. They are also the hallmarks of prosperous nations and successful corporate entities. Wealth is, simply put, an accumulation of resources. A wealthy (or rich) individual, community, or nation has more resources than a poor one.

Power is the ability to exert control over one's environment or other entities. Both wealth and power are intimately tied to societal structures cultures.

Some people have wealth that is unimaginable to the rest of us and the gap between rich and poor is widening year after year. Closing the gap or trying to answer the question is not a simple act.

Consider the fact that wealth and poverty have been shifting over time. Families with very unequal distribution of incomes are mostly the poor and incomes are often more evenly distributed to the wealthy.

Often defined purely the status, wealth relates to one's capacity to engage easily and productively in society. This means "having enough money to fulfill basic needs: food, adequate shelter, basic healthcare, and education. Economic security is connected to employment.

Having access to adequate pay and stable work makes for security. With this security come many privileges that people sometimes take for granted.

What some see as security for the wealthy the same translate to access to credit and loans that lead to the opposite of wealth: debt. The debt load at an individual level can be paralyzing; it affects decision making, thereby limiting choices.

The Influencer

Chapter 1

Insanity

This book will not be about the thousands of social media influencers or celebrity influencers. Instead, I want to focus on wealth creation and how you can change the next generation financially. What I hope to accomplish is something that will resonate with my readers that will start a new process.

I am under the impression that you have at least read "Wealth Creation The Mindset" and are now on to this next level of knowledge. I believe a form of insanity affects the mindset in a way that causes one to want what others have and not want to do the work.

One definition of insanity is continuing to do the same thing in the same way, but expecting a different result. This is the case with most of us, change is hard, and change is perceived as difficult. With that in mind, in a time when wealth creation is at the lowest it has ever been, why are we still trying to motivate with money when it hasn't been successful?

What do I mean by "still trying to motivate with money", you will not accomplish wealth creation simply if the thought of money itself is the influencer. While we all love the idea of earning and saving, it is unclear why we continue to spend countless dollars trying to motivate and engage ourselves with monetary incentives if we know it doesn't work. It does allow us to feel good temporarily while being able to say I tried.

Insanity

Over the next few chapters, I am going to try and place what I believe will be a life-changing and fundamental influencer from three different angles Autonomy, Mastery, and Purpose. I am hopeful that this stage will be the light in the darkness for you.

I believe that all people are motivated by at least one of these and often a combination of the three. Interestingly, money is not on this list. While I believe people are initially motivated by money, if you pay them enough to meet their needs, money becomes less and less effective over time. It’s just like an affirmation without action, empty.

Here comes trouble… I never understood why someone would post on social media daily good morning millionaire and not make a single action toward the habits of a true millionaire. Insanity!

I wish I could tell you that incentives and threats work. You can't offer incentives and make someone motivated for wealth creation. All you can do is provide an environment where they can tap into what is already inside of them.

Is it praise, recognition, serving a greater purpose, becoming a subject matter expert, or something entirely different? An influencer will not influence if what's being offered is not important to the individual.

The idea of money alone can't buy wealth creation. Wealth creation comes from feeling valued and appreciated, having a positive opinion about your journey, and being clear on what contribution you will make to the overall success of the goals. It's most critical at the immediate wealth creation level, that your values dictate results more than any other factor.

Money itself does not make better savers or investors, but personal development can. If personal development is so critical to your success, why aren't more people investing in development instead of Starbucks?

Investing in the right development program can provide a significantly higher ROI. Common sense isn't always common practice.

Developing yourself and ensuring family members are clear about their roles and responsibilities improve earning and savings, morale, and engagement in wealth creation. Creating an influencing climate takes time, effort, and energy. It has to be a deliberate effort.

I'm not suggesting that money should never be used as an influencer. Some people perform best with incentives—but not everyone does. Some people crave opportunities for investing, some thrive on financial management, and some desire the opportunity growth wealth.

Spending time trying to identify what influences you and then finding meaningful ways to make those things happen might not be the easiest strategy, but it is consistently more successful than the alternative. And it can bring lasting results.

Insanity

People universally crave respect, peace of mind, success, recognition, financial stability, admiration, and love. These are the influencers that stick—the ones that can spur people to commit, take risks, and change behaviors.

I want to establish a vision of the insanity of doing the same things over and over expecting a different result. Wealth creation for so many has never occurred because of such insanity. Some people constantly self-sabotage their opportunity for wealth creation by talking themselves out of any chance of opportunity.

Regardless of the source of the information, they seem to discover or should I say identify a way to hinder the potential to accomplish something new. Even if it means an upgrade from their current environment, they still find roadblocks. This is much different from what I will talk about in chapter 5 Behavior. This is insanity.

However, I am going to try and guide those of you who are constantly setting up roadblocks, hurdles, and mountains that hinder you and provide you with new approaches and insight.

First, it's all good reading about ways to get ahead in life, but no account will ever reach you in quite the same way as having something that you can envision and relate to.

I often speak about my own experiences because I know that every single aspect of my life is relatable to others. There are many ways for you to relate to the experiences of others WHO can move you and inspire you to make your own dreams come true.

So, let's put insanity to bed, this is about influence. I want to fill you with drive and determination to reach your full potential, and not let anything stand in your way. I am talking about wealth creation and generational wealth. Can I make you want to grab life with both hands and go for what you want, whatever it is?

Most people have done all that they're ever going to do – they raise a family, they earn a living, and then they die. I am not trying to be disrespectful, but every time I return to my home people are standing on the same corner, doing the same things as 20 years ago.

Work, live, and die. That's what we're supposed to do, right? Wrong! Life is made for greater things, and you are meant for greater things. Wealth Creation is one of them.

Picture you permitting yourself to rise above other people's opinions, break free of their prejudices, and see your money invested in a new way. Like now, you are taking new first steps towards following your own passion and making your dream come true.

There are so many things that impact what influences you, stress doesn't come from the real facts, stress comes from the meaning that we give the facts. "I don't see how this little money is going to make a difference." The fact that I ask you to save $20 a week, you bad-mouth it with that type of statement.

It is about you. Life is about your choices. Every day you are faced with hundreds of choices many of them are repeated choices. You need to snap out of this insanity and trust that better choices will change old conditions that once shaped your life.

I know we are early in this book, but I want you to take a moment now to pause and reflect on some choices you have made in the past, and think about the direction your life took because of them, both good and bad.

How much money would I have saved, only if? How long would I have been a homeowner? What would my 401K look like? See, you know that you have the choice to focus on what you want and that when you focus, you can achieve whatever we want.

Now that is the title of the next book in this series Wealth Creation "The Focus".

We all tend to waste time, but if you have a goal if you have a raging passion that rages away to make sure that everything you do propels you forward then don't be afraid to fail. Every step that you take gets you closer to accomplishing the goal to turn this goal – this vision – into reality.

I would like to remind you that your conviction and your convenience don't live on the same block. Neither does your confidence, you may have to be willing to leave everything and everyone behind to grow into the version of yourself that you know you want.

Insanity, doing and being the same way over and over again, when is that moment that you vow to yourself never to be that broke or that broken again? Change, success, drive…they're all inconvenient and disruptive. Let me tell you that on the other side of disruption is your discovery. What once held you back was not meant to break you, it was meant to build you.

Another part of the insanity that gets overlooked but often influences you is the environment that you are in. If you don't take control of your environment, it takes control of you. Guess what, you are in control of your environment whether you realize it or not, what goes on around you has a massive influence on the way you feel and the way you act.

When you take on the leadership of your own life, you can defy outside influences and set your tone for the day ahead, regardless of whatever or whoever is exerting pressure from the outside.

I triple double dare you to take 10 minutes for yourself at the start of every day – for gratitude, prayer or wishes for family and friends, and a recap of what you want to accomplish that day, and your day will continue on that same path of thankfulness, hope, and goals. You must do this for 30 consecutive days, with no exception.

Listen your mind doesn't know the difference between something you vividly imagined and something real, literally! What the mind can conceive and believe, it can/will achieve. As much as this applies to positive things, it also can be applied to negative things, so if you imagine failure, that's what you will get. Fill your mind with thoughts of success and that's what will happen. None of these habits are difficult to accomplish, but in doing so you will change your entire mindset into one of a hugely successful person, no matter what you want to achieve in life.

There are a lot of sharks in the world; if you hope to complete the swim, you will have to deal with them. So if you want to change your world, don't back down from the sharks. The world is full of people who want to bring you down (the sharks) but if you stand your ground, they will eventually swim away, leaving you to go on to bigger and better things.

Immerse yourself in this and find words of wisdom, and take that next step into your best life. It is impossible to live without failing at something unless you live so cautiously that you might as well not have lived at all. In which case, you fail by default.

Chapter Two

Self-Determine -Your First Influencer

I believe that one of your biggest influencers is yourself. However, I accept the fact that there are many other parts to the process. Wealth creation is a mission it's a desire that is nested in the heart of the discoverer. Wealth Creation is the balance of two, the heart and the mind.

For you to accomplish the concept of you having the ability to make choices and manage your own life it is important to have self-determination.

In the book The Mindset I talked about this being mental, self-determination is the ability that plays an important role in your psychological health and well-being. Self-determination allows you to feel that you have control over your choices and lives.

Your motivation is off the chart when you are feeling that what you do will affect the outcome whenever you take action. Listen, your self-determination already causes a major impact on a wide variety of areas including education, work, parenting, exercise, and health. Strange enough I did not mention money or wealth creation.

I will suspect that you may become influenced to grow and change when your needs for competence, connection, and autonomy are fulfilled. If I am clear here with the basic concept that allows you to engage in activities for the essential rewards of wealth creation itself, it will prove to be awesome.

Like most things, we tend to be driven by a need to grow and gain fulfillment. The need for growth drives behavior. Think about the time when your best friend called you and told you about a trip to one of your favorite places.

This trip is expensive and you would have to work overtime and a part-time job to get the resources for this trip. Your behavior changes almost immediately.

You can actively show your mastery over challenges and take in new experiences that are essential for developing a cohesive sense of self or your desire.

The fact that this action came from a behavior motivated by a friend takes away your self-determination or does it. It is not a part of the same energy anyway.

You need to feel in control of your behaviors and goals. This sense of being able to take direct action that will result in real change plays a major part in helping you feel self-determined.

Many of you believe you need to gain mastery of tasks and learn different skills. That is important because when you feel that you have the skills needed for success, you are more likely to take actions that will help them achieve goals.

Imagine you had failed at setting a budget or even saving money. If you have high self-determination, you will admit your fault, believe that you can do something to fix the problem, and take action to correct the mistake.

But, and I say but if you have low self-determination, you might instead look for other things that you can blame. You will make excuses, assign blame, or refuse to admit your role.

Most importantly, perhaps, is that you won't feel motivated to fix the mistake. Instead, you might feel helpless to control the situation and believe that nothing that you do will have any real effect.

It is important to realize that the psychological growth that is developing by your self-determination does not simply happen automatically.

Your growth and development are either proactive or passive and are largely influenced by the social conditions in which you are raised. Through our relationships and interactions with others, we can either foster or thwart well-being and personal growth.

As I talk about your behavior becoming increasingly controlled by outside influences, you can begin to feel less in control of your behavior and your desire is diminished.

However, sometimes outside influences can offer unexpected positive encouragement, and feedback on your performance can increase your desire.

Self-Determine

This helps you to feel more competent, which is one of the key needs for personal growth. Our learned behavior is complex at times and you are rarely driven to act by a single source of influence. You may often draw on multiple sources of influence in the pursuit of a goal.

Having variations of influences can also fuel a degree of engagement in actions because you feel you have some level of personal control and the behaviors ultimately align with something important for self-concept.

Your self-determination can play an important role in how you function in many different areas of your life. Feeling in control can help you feel more committed, passionate, interested, and satisfied with the things that you have to do for the journey of wealth creation.

Those of you "WHO" feel that you can have a positive effect on wealth creation will feel more engaged and motivated or influenced. You must foster this sense of self-determination by allowing yourself to take an active role and responsibilities in meaningful encouragement of yourself.

Those of you "WHO" feel that you are capable of achieving your goals and overcoming challenges are expected to be driven to perform much better.

Excelling in small steps of wealth creation allows you to gain an important sense of competence and build mastery in skills that are enjoyable and important to you on this journey.

Listen, your self-determination can also play an important role in all of your social relationships. A sense of belongingness is critical in the development of self-determination. Forging close, affectionate relationships with other people will improve self-determination and influence.

Always seek positive relationships with people who will support you in the pursuit of your goals. Wealth creation is not a goal and desire for everyone.

To strengthen your self-determination, it is helpful to think about what a highly self-determined individual might look like. Believe that you have control over your own lives.

You do have an internal locus of control and know that your behaviors will influence outcomes. When confronted with challenges, you know that you can overcome them through diligence, good choices, and hard work.

You do not rely on external rewards or punishments to influence you to take action. You engage in deliberate behaviors because they are good at helping set goals and work toward those aims.

Always base your actions on your own goals and behaviors. In other words, you are intentionally engaging in actions that you know will bring them closer to your goals of wealth creation.

Never dismiss responsibility for your behaviors. It's okay to take credit for your success, but also accept the blame for moments of setbacks. If you do fail and you will, it is okay, you are constantly improving self-awareness, decision-making skills, self-regulation, and goal-setting abilities that can encourage the g**rowth of a stronger you. "WHO?"**

Becoming skilled in areas that are important to you is a helpful way to build your sense of influence. You must have a strong interest in money management, savings, and investing learn as much as you can about it, and improve your skills so you can be more competent in ("WHO") you. The more you learn and practice, the more skilled and an influencer you will feel like.

Personal Money Map Month:________

My Needs Descriptions	Planned Spending	Actual Spending
1. ____________________	$ __________	$__________
2. ____________________	$ __________	$__________
3. ____________________	$ __________	$__________
4. ____________________	$ __________	$__________
5. ____________________	$ __________	$__________
6. ____________________	$ __________	$__________

My Total Needs $ __________ $__________

My Wants Descriptions	Planned Spending	Actual Spending
1. ____________________	$ __________	$__________
2. ____________________	$ __________	$__________
3. ____________________	$ __________	$__________
4. ____________________	$ __________	$__________
5. ____________________	$ __________	$__________

Chapter Three

Mental Programming

No way. Right? Yes, way. There is a form of conditioning that is established at birth. The first stage is a critical part of your overall development. It set in motion your learning, and ability to speak, walk, talk and eat, it also expands to sight words and books.

It establishes many of your core beliefs. It's no wonder why you are not wealth-minded and focused on wealth creation. It's a part of our being, that part that has you set in your ways.

Our parents would never consciously choose to set limits or to limit our options and thoughts and potential. And yet they do so, unconsciously, unknowingly, and unintentionally, every day. You set these same unconsciously, unknowingly, and unintentionally limits on yourself as well. It's learned behavior.

The degree to which mental programming constricts your life and creativity is the extent to which you are unaware of its control over you, or, unwilling to change it. I want to point this out so that you can come back and revisit it.

Two key differences between positive and negative influences will respond to the programming as you seek to change: positive influences amplify change while negative influences reduce change.

We are all running on an operating system installed by our family and associations, beliefs, and assumptions. Even to what we can describe as the invisible chains of conditioning, your freedom from this is going, to begin with, your awareness.

How you feel about wealth creation, wealthy people, investing and savings are the results of our upbringing. You can walk around completely in the dark as to why you like Rent-2-

Own over owning outright. It's how you were raised there is no value to it so it just seems normal. It's not…

Check this, I know you all heard about how an elephant is trained to be restrained by a chain that it could easily break. The elephant is trained from infancy to know that the chain binds it. The conditioning is so complete for so long that as the elephant grows, it never thinks to question or oppose that which keeps it bound.

It accepts what the training as real, though what was real for the baby elephant would not hold true for the grown elephant. It's the same with our beliefs. We are conditioned to believe in the personal and cultural constraints that keep us from becoming all that we can be.

As it relates to finance, most, never break free of that invisible chain. Wealth creation and financial freedom are more likely to live on the leading edge of failure. And yet, a poverty mindset constantly labors under the haze of a twists reality.

Think about this for a moment. Have you ever heard any of these — or similar — terms, of common programmed mindsets, I'm not good enough, I have writer's block, I am a starving artist, I can't get a publisher, I'm too old to…, I'm too young to…, I don't know how to ________, now you can understand programming impact.

There is a path to freedom from Programming Influencers. But I want to be clear as to why I am talking about this as one of your influencers. Your ability to pursue wealth and create wealth and build a solid legacy for your next generation begins with the awareness to probe and question your indoctrinations.

Be they religious, political, societal, financial, or about your perception of your health and personal abilities. You must break free. Accept that you are a product of your environment and that much of what you think to construct your reality. —

This is the moment, this is the moment that you have become aware and now it is time to create a new life by pushing past the boundaries that have kept you from reaching the next level that you aspire to reach. Ask Yourself:

1. Do limiting beliefs run through my head?
2. What beliefs no longer serve me?
3. If this belief (that is holding me back) didn't exist, what might I do?
4. What is an old story I often repeat to anyone new?
5. Does it uplift me or keep me bound?
6. Is it an excuse for why I'm not yet where I want to be?
7. Is it something from my past that has no business in my future?

No one likes to think of themselves in bondage or prison in their mindset, but programming that you get from your upbringing is simply the conditioning of the invisible prison of mental programming that can keep you trapped in limited thinking, not just about money.

Do not think are believe it's all negative, no not all conditioning is negative. Some programming is necessary for your survival and functioning in society. Mindset training, for example, is essential for reinforcing your aspirations and determination to achieve your goals and dreams.

Every culture has its norms, and some might be the opposite. For instance, to burp loudly at the table may be considered by most to be rude in some households, whereas it's expected in others and considered a tribute to the meal and the cook. LOL (I know I learned that at my house)

Programming

Make no mistake about it things can be a little confusing though, we are at the crossroads where every day norms are being challenged by younger generations.

Norms such as "respect your elders", "don't question authority", and "what will people think", aren't embraced by younger generations as much as by our parents and grandparents who grew up in an era where that was automatic and assumed.

Wealth creation has not always been readily available as it is today. Conditions that held back our parents are not roadblocks today. As times change, there are conflicts between the old and new as older ways that might be antiquated are cast aside, leaving a generational gap.

Children are still squeezed in between traditionalism hidden as "what will people think", typically introduced by their parents, and peer pressure to "fit in".

As with many things, there's no one way that is right and the other way wrong. Rather, there is truth and benefit in it all. Your task now as a seeker of wealth creation, is to discern the conditioning that serves you and that which doesn't. To do so requires self-awareness and openly inquiring objectivity.

I spoke earlier about how limited conditioning set back your programming. Intentional feelings and thoughts about money and wealth, even wealthy people impact you. Is it not funny that we feel a certain way about people "WHO" we like to become? Time to break free of limiting conditioning is essential to becoming more of all that you can be.

The first book of this series The Mindset is an example of powerful and positive programming essential for reinforcing your aspirations and determination to achieve your goals and dreams. The power of visioning is proven to be highly effective when employed daily and followed by action.

Visioning creates a blueprint which is then constructed and reinforced through goal setting, focus, and action. The next book of this series is "The Focus" once you begin to unravel the layers of conditioning constricting your life, you become increasingly aware of the extent to which it is limiting you. Impressions, thoughts, reactions, and decisions are all a part of your conditioning.

Conditioning impacts the way you experience your life… and you are operating through layers of conditioning. However, not all conditioning is negative. Some conditions are necessary for survival and functioning in our current society.

Most people live their entire lives completely unaware of the degree to which they're influenced by the indoctrination of others (programming).

However, no matter your programming in life thus far, no matter at what age and no matter your income level changing limiting conditioning are essential to creating the wealth you desire.

Living a wealthy life begins with breaking free of indoctrination and societal memes that negatively influence you from the outside in. Say this three times please "The Outside In".

You are conditioned by your environment and indoctrinated from birth as to the truth of these beliefs. And so for you, it would be true, and that belief would condition all that you think and do. I understand that these are sensitive topics.

You tend to hold your beliefs near and dear to your identity. Often they form and inform your identity.

However… If we are to continue growing in consciousness, we need to push the boundaries of the belief that may be limiting our lives.

It's the same with your beliefs. You are conditioned to believe in the personal and cultural constraints that keep us from becoming all that we can be. Your freedom begins with the awareness to probe and question your indoctrinations.

As I mentioned earlier, be it religious, political, societal, financial, or about your perception of your health and personal abilities, for you to break free is to first become aware that you are a product of your environment.

Freedom begins with the courage to question yourself and your beliefs. Become curious as a child and ask, 'Why?'

Keep on asking 'Why?' All the days of your life keep growing and learning.

As you mature, you have more freedom to explore, discover and decide your beliefs from the inside out and to question what doesn't make sense. The challenge is that as you age, you tend to become more rigid, more fixed in mindset, and more "set in your ways".

There is a difference between becoming confident and definite while remaining open to growth. You can become definite about your purpose to grow and evolve. You can become definite about change.

The moment we say, "I've never been…", or "I can't…", or "Those people are…", and other limiting beliefs, you close the door of opportunity and turn away from the possibility to learn, grow and understand.

You turn away from the chance to love as well because with understanding comes compassion and empathy, and with that comes greater love.

Live the life of your choosing, not of your conditioning… creating yourself from the inside out, begins with awareness. Do not become set in your ways. Buildings are set, concrete is set, but people? We are living organisms destined to grow… all the days of our lives.

Release mental programming that's holding you back from your greater success, happiness, and joy. Oh let's not forget why you are reading this, Wealth Creation.

Now that you have examined ideas around mental programming, it's important to conclude with a consideration of the health of your brain itself.

What if you awakened today with no limiting beliefs? No past traumas… no ill health holding you back… no ill will or hurt for or from anyone? What if your mind was filled with possibility and gratitude, enthusiasm and joy?

You would be lighter, happier, and more free to CREATE today… to laugh and love and rejoice and be grateful for the blessings you do have.

And now condition yourself to start the process of Wealth Creation.

Many things can have an impact on you and can influence your ability to be successful. Having good energy levels are directly correlated to what motivation, stamina and positivity goes along with of the crucial things to help you to achieve and maintain wealth creation.

The goal is to make wealth creation work every day of the week. Find yourself a routine that does it and stay with it. It's also important to give your mind and emotions time off to heal. If you're not a morning person it can be counterproductive to schedule your financials or wealth creation for early morning.

Make sure you find a surrounding in a place that motivates you. That can be in a park, on a beach, at work, or in your own home. If you like your surroundings you'll not only be more likely to keep with your focus but you will, more than likely, perform better as well with wealth creation.

Chapter Four

Am I The Controller

Wealth creation you will find is not just about the influence it is also about relationships. But, in this section, I am going to talk about control. "Who" does not want control? Have you ever come across a controlling personality? Or perhaps you've never known that you're dealing with one? What are the personality traits of a person of this nature, and how is one to deal with that?

Wait, are you a controlling person?

You may question the way I go about this conversation and the impact that it may have on your wealth creation. I want you to be sure that you understand that a controlling personality will ruin perfectly normal relationships. So imagine losing connections that can place you in places you would not get to without relationships.

If you desire wealth creation, this space is not designed for the weak-minded. It demands a fine balance from you and expects you to comply with the conditions outlined in your pursuit of wealth. In that way it wants you to learn to be generous and open and willing to adjust with everyone around.

Ideally, you are to give each person his/her own space and respect their preferences, choices, and decisions. Now there are times when you want something done your way, and your way alone, for whatever reasons—logical or otherwise.

Control

Sometimes you are not open to adjustments and compromises. But at most other times, you are flexible… except you just aren't. You are not willing to make any adjustments and do not provide any space for the other. You have a controlling personality type. A controlling personality, as the name suggests, is a personality type that needs to be in control at all times—a control freak so to say.

While you tend to exert control in certain situations, some do nothing but that… all the time. Imagine dealing with a controlling person who controls every small thing that you do.

Needless to say, a manipulative personality such as this one puts a lot of pressure on people around them and makes adjustments for everyone difficult. In extremities, it can turn into a controlling personality disorder and thereby making it difficult for others who are in controlling relationships as well.

Being controlling can be a deflator or an influencer, if you chose to exert your control on your finances and money management it serves as an influencer.

However, you can become that other person, that control freak, and not advance beyond where you are currently. By now you should understand that there are a lot of processes that are personally related that impact your wealth creation.

The danger with the personality trait of a controller is something you need to identify early in this process of your transition. How would you ever know if a person or yourself is controlling or not? When you discover people living in constant fear and unease that whatever they do will set the other person off or you have to gauge their mood before saying or doing anything.

I am going to keep saying this. We want to have what the one we dislike has. Controlling people will control everything, however miniature—like the control of the remote.

They employ manipulative techniques and keep on and on about something that they want to be done their way until the other person gives in. They then act as if the other person has finally taken the correct decision.

I have a client who is in the constant company of a controlling person who often feels frustrated and run down and feels like they have lost control over their own lives. There is constant criticism doled out for every small thing. They put others down to feel superior and boost their ego.

All of this deeply impacts your ability for wealth creation as well as other areas of your life. As I stated earlier, control has both positive and negative affect.

Taking a controlling behavior in relationships often involves people with a volatile temper who might even resort to physical abuse like twisting your arm and slapping you.

They are bothered at your confidence by criticizing whatever you do, putting you down, making you feel useless and dumb, at fault for doing the things that you enjoy doing, and even dressing or looking a particular way. Thus low self-esteem develops and a person begins to feel that he/she 'deserves' to be treated that way.

There is something else about controlling individuals they will try and isolate you from friends and family so that no one can influence your thoughts other than them. They'll abuse and accuse your family and friends and question you endlessly about your motives. Eventually, you are cut off from any support allowing them to control you exclusively.

People do not realize that they are controlled by others. It is often so indirect that by the time they realize it they are not themselves. Some people are broke only because someone else controls them.

These control freaks never own up or take responsibility for their actions and behavior. It is always someone else's fault. They are so smooth with it that they will discourage you from indulging in any other activities that they cannot control, like any areas of interest and wealth creation that do not include them.

They will either criticize it till they force you to give it up or accompany you to it or make you miserable, thus forcing you to quit.

A controller will always put the onus on the other person in the business relationship, the personal relationship, saying that whatever they did was never enough.

Remember, they often make comments like

"No one can take me for granted", "I don't take no for an answer" or "I always get things done my way". All these statements reek of control.

One of the more common controls freak symptoms also includes a person who is often moody and is easily angered with normal questions. They never compliment or praise you for what you do. Instead, they often suggest that it was not because of your talent that it happened, that an external force of some kind was at play. Okay, okay…

Listen a controller has no respect of person. As I stated earlier, I believe there is a positive and negative trait to a controlling personality, it's not easy to deal with. It's as if you are constantly under pressure to be something you are not, to be afraid, and careful. That is why it becomes important to recognize the signs of a controlling person and learn how to deal with them. Including yourself.

You should always reaffirm to yourself that you are not anything less than the others just because someone tells you that. Always stand firm on your ground that you will not relent and be mistreated or held back.

It's okay to stand up to them and tell them that you are feeling stressed out and controlled, that you are not happy with where things are and going. Make sure they know that they cannot control your every move like one would a child.

Control

It is important to try and communicate with them and not to them as they do to you. This is where you become the controller by taking up all your lost hobbies and interests and investment goals. Get back control of your life. At the end of the day, your peace of mind is prime. Is it not?

Speaking of your peace of mind is important that you remember your likes to be in charge and be in control of your environment, if not you need to be. You have to be very goal-oriented and practical in your solutions, especially with wealth creation.

You being in control makes you your own influencer and as you arrive at some of your solutions and goals it will entail a no-nonsense, bottom-line approach.

You become the director of the best play in your life. You have the strengths to embrace changes as they happen. Your journey towards wealth creation is all about you being in control and taking charge of the vision that will guide you. Even with the right mindset, you will be faced with a fast-paced environment requiring you to be in control.

I am a controller I like to set up the atmosphere around me. I love working with other controllers that have many of the same qualities as I do. Could just be my own opinion (lol), but a controller is great to work with but more importantly, really inspires you with enthusiasm and creativity.

Let me walk you through the process of understanding this differently than those around you. You see, just like with the mindset you are having a new perspective on many of the basic things that you once ignored or never connected with. One of my mentors always reminds me that there are things I don't know that I don't know.

As a controller for your wealth creation, you need to have a clear vision of what you are attempting to create. You must know in advance what are your most important aims or goals, what you want to create, and why you want to create them. Whilst it's up to the purposes of the household and legacy how the mission comes into existence, knowing your core vision, inside and out, is the single most important item for a great controller.

Originality is not for everyone and yes I said it out loud. A truly great controller needs to create something new. It may be through the bringing together of ideas previously formed, even by other people. It may be through seeing another's idea through a different lens.

It may be the level of polish and precision that is brought to the vision, or the tools used to tell the different story. Either way, originality is key to a controller's greatness. You only need to change or modify the wheel not recreate it.

When you consider influencers, are they not Inspiring and passionate and looked upon as a leader? You the controller must be completely invested and enthused in your vision, and you must be able to inspire and enthuse others about it. It's no good having an amazing idea for your household but being unable to bring others in to follow that idea to inception and completion.

As a controller, you not only have to have a clear, original vision but inspire others to follow that dream with you as you create it.

One of the next books is "Wealth Creation The Trust" and that book is going to echo the influencer because you as the controller must trust your team of resources to bring the vision to life. By laying out the clear, original vision in an inspiring way, you will then take a step back to allow the creation of the resources to bring their unique talents to bear on the vision.

You will ideally assemble a team you have complete faith in and will show that by allowing that team free (to a point, you are still in control) reign to bring the wealth creation goals to life in the ways they're inspired to.

From a purely practical stance, you do not have to be experienced in finance or money management to be a controller in this area. You have to change that mindset and have looked at your options and decided to work with solid skills based on your recent learning to support your vision, originality, passion, and faith. All of this ties together for a larger purpose.

Do not get it twisted, you must objectively be open to other people's ideas/points of view (but absolutely, unwaveringly certain of your own.

Being inspiring and leading others is totally up for new ideas you may not have thought of before – in fact, you should welcome it! This is the central point of wealth creation. It's all in the name – the controller influences – you guide the process, course correcting now and then but very much open to any new creative endeavors that serve your overall vision and goal.

See being a controller or influencer is not all that bad. You must be tactful and constructively receive criticism. This is one where my opinion may diverge from the norm. I am absolute of the mindset that any feedback, no matter how critical, can always be delivered with tact – politely, civilly, and with constructive intention.

Similarly, it's up to the creative to receive that feedback in the manner it was intended – not personally, but as a course, correction to put everyone back on the path to that central, defining, original vision. You are still the visionary

Many years ago, I use to go into elementary schools in Atlanta, GA, and teach a program Saving Is Fun to the children. Saving, investing and wealth creation must be fun. Again – this may only be my opinion, but there has to be some fun in the process of this life-changing process.

Fun is a subjective term, though; from my point of view, the fun comes from really getting to grips with the vision and crafting that into something you are proud of, that fulfills the brief and then some through a collaborative venture, where your

A-game and skills are on the table. Some cheerfulness in the process doesn't go amiss though, especially during growth.

Stay focussed on the goals, Wealth Creation "The Focus" is another book in the series, do not be easily distracted. You can't be swayed from the task at hand. When you are frustrated, the market crashing, it moving slowly, your friends well you know… you must stay the course until the job is done. I've seen this unwavering focus trickle down into the people quitting, similarly, I've seen a somewhat-distracted person go into depression. You set the tone. You must be the WHO in control here.

Your level of focus is a signifier of how important the goals are to them watching you. Distraction = low priority, if the mission is not important enough to keep your attention, why should the family invest anything more?

Finally, always have a few good ideas ready to go when this one is finished. While you are focused on the goal level at hand, you should always have the next level, or even a slate of them, ready to go, at various stages of wealth creation.

Perhaps this isn't the most obvious quality of a controller, but for me, it signifies the breadth of ideas the influencer has: you aren't just a one-trick pony. One-and-done isn't in your vocabulary; you are in it for the long haul. Right?

Chapter Five

The Behavior

The behavioral wealth effect is my theory suggesting that people spend more as the value of their assets rises or appears to rise. The idea is that people feel more financially secure and confident about their wealth when their homes or investment portfolios increase in value. They are made to feel richer, even if their income and fixed costs are the same as before.

Let me break this down to make it clear. When most people that are meeting their monthly obligations and then make the final payment on their car, are now left with $465.00, instead of the first notion is to spend it, not save or invest.

I have long said that I have clients who earn enough money to meet all of their monthly obligations and more. However, they often see their income as their wealth and find financial security in that fact alone.

If you are somewhat successful financially, meaning that you have the income to meet your needs, likely, your behavioral effect with money is not truly maximized in the area of saving and investing that I will talk more about in this chapter.

In an ideal world, people would always make optimal decisions that provide them with the greatest benefit and satisfaction. When people are presented with various options under the conditions of lack, they would choose the option that maximizes their satisfaction.

I assume that most people, given their preferences and constraints, are capable of making rational decisions by effectively weighing the costs and benefits of each option available to them. The final decision made will be the best choice for them.

See now, a rational person should have self-control and is unmoved by emotions and external factors and, hence, knows what is best for himself. Some people are not rational and are incapable of making good financial decisions.

I do not know why people sometimes make irrational decisions, and why and how their behavior does not follow the predictions of what most believe to be normal.

In our normal lives, we make decisions such as how much to pay for a cup of coffee, whether to go to graduate school, whether to pursue a healthy lifestyle, how much to contribute towards retirement, etc. these are the decisions that most people make at some point in their lives.

The effect of behavioral choices creates the why we use to decide to go for choice A, instead of choice B.

Because we are emotional and easily distracted beings, people make decisions that are not in their self-interest. For example, if Mr. Jones wants to lose weight and is equipped with information about the number of calories available in each edible product, he will opt only for the food products with minimal calories.

Because we as people are influenced by our behavioral impact that even if Mr. Jones wants to lose weight and sets his mind on eating healthy food going forward, his end behavior will be subject to cognitive bias, emotions, and social influences.

If a commercial on TV advertises a brand of ice cream at an attractive price and quotes that all human beings need 2,000 calories a day to function effectively, after all, the mouth-watering ice cream image, price, and seemingly valid statistics may lead Mr. Jones to fall into the sweet temptation and fall off of the weight loss bandwagon, showing his lack of self-control.

The behavioral action of most people is the use of rules of thumb or mental shortcuts to make a quick decision. However, when the decision is made leads to error, which can lead to cognitive bias. People's decisions to make irrational choices like personal finance can explain why investors make rash decisions when trading in the capital markets.

If, I said if you look at how companies are increasingly incorporating the behavioral effect to increase sales of their products. Just consider that on January 9, 2007, the iPhone was introduced for $600 and quickly reduced to $400.

What if the basic value of the phone was $400 anyway? If Apple introduced the phone for $400, the initial reaction to the price in the smartphone market might have been negative as the phone might be thought to be too pricey. But by introducing the phone at a higher price and bringing it down to $400, consumers believed they were getting a pretty good deal and sales surged for Apple.

Also, consider a soap manufacturer who produces the same soap but markets them in two different packages to appeal to multiple target groups. One package advertises the soap for all soap users, the other for consumers with sensitive skin.

The latter target would not have purchased the product if the package did not specify that the soap was for sensitive skin. We opt for the soap with the sensitive skin label even though it's the same product in the general package.

Many things are promoted to us in this way, because of our mental shortcuts and rules of thumb we make what appear to be rational decisions quickly having our emotions impacting the decision.

But when it comes to money and investing, we are not always as rational as we think we are. Are we? Being one of those rational actors, who never make the mistake of believing that your individuals behave rationally and that all choices that you make result in outcomes aligned with your own best interests

Here I go with labels on people. What I am trying to point out is that we are both rational and irrational people and some behaviors influence how we respond to financial situations. You do not have to agree with me at all.

Okay consider this, rational people make these rational choices based on error-free calculations given complete information that is always available to them. Rational people thus try to actively maximize their advantage in any situation and consistently try to minimize their losses in a self-interested manner. Does this possibly sound like anybody that you may know?

There is a big impact with our behavioral finance that somehow have to understand that our emotions influence our financial and investment decision-making processes.

Fear of regret, or simply regret, with our emotional reaction everyday people experience after realizing they've made an error in judgment. Faced with the prospect of selling a stock, we become emotionally affected by the price at which they purchased the stock. So, they avoid selling it as a way to avoid the regret of having made a bad investment, as well as the embarrassment of reporting a loss. We all hate to be wrong, don't we?

I remember coaching a financial class and we were discussing stocks and the price of stocks. We decided that this one petroleum stock would take off. I purchased 1000 shares at 0.23 a share, with fees that cost me $239.00. Weeks later this stock was up to $27.86 a share, the data paid off, and I made a rational decision based on the information I had.

An investment that cost $239 is now valued at $27,860. Great news right? NO! The SEC froze trading of the stock. That means no further trading and the company ordered a reverse split. What? What does all this mean?

The next morning I had a new total of stock that I now own, the split was a 23-1 negative split, and for every 23 shares I have 1 share, this left me with 44 total shares now valued at $1226. Regret and fear are real.

However, unlike most of my associates “WHO” purchased this stock sold, I did not and as I write this book, the market value of the stock is $87.49 giving my total shares of 44 valued at $3849 which does not hurt as much anymore.

As an investor, you should ask yourself when contemplating selling a stock: "What are the consequences of repeating the same purchase if this security were already liquidated, and would I invest in it again?" If the answer is "no," it's time to sell; otherwise, the result is regret in buying a losing stock and the regret of not selling when it became clear that a poor investment decision was made—and a vicious cycle ensues where avoiding regret leads to more regret.

Regret can also hold true for investors when they discover that a stock they had only considered buying has increased in value. I really hate this mindset in people who are close to me or who have been following me for years, sitting on a watch list of stocks that are having tremendous growth and doing nothing about it.

Some investors avoid the possibility of feeling this regret by following the conventional wisdom and buying only stocks that everyone else is buying, rationalizing their decision with "everyone else is doing it."

Oddly enough, many people feel much less embarrassed about losing money on a popular stock that half the world owns than about losing money on an unknown or unpopular stock. CRAZY…

This is like Chapter One - The Mental in the book "The Mindset", there is a tendency to place particular events into mental compartments, and the difference between these compartments sometimes impacts the behavior more than the events themselves.

Here is a good example of just that, you aim to catch a show at the local theater and tickets are $20 each. When you get there, you realize you've lost a $20 bill. Do you buy a $20 ticket for the show anyway? There are studies out there that show roughly 88% of people in a similar situation would do so.

Now, let's say you paid for the $20 ticket in advance. When you arrive at the door, you realize your ticket is at home. Would you pay $20 to purchase another? Only 40% of people would buy another ticket. Notice, however, that in both scenarios, you're out $40: different scenarios, the same amount of money, different mental compartments. Pretty silly, huh? I AM JUST SAYING

Listen, your behavior towards wealth creation involves your mental ability in how you account for your investing an example is best illustrated by the hesitation to sell an investment that once had monstrous gains and now has a modest gain.

During an economic boom and bull market, people get accustomed to healthy, albeit paper, gains. When the market correction deflates investors' net worth, they're more hesitant to sell at a smaller profit margin. They create mental compartments for the gains they once had, causing them to wait for the return of that profitable period.

I am someone who does this more than I want to admit. I promise you that it doesn't take a rocket science to know that people prefer a sure investment return to an uncertain one—we want to get paid for taking on any extra risk. That's pretty reasonable. Here's the strange part. Most people will express a different degree of emotion towards gains than towards losses. Individuals are more stressed by prospective losses than they are happy from equal gains.

I have a business partner named Dr. Copeland, he has a Ph.D. in money, we oftentimes discuss consumers' behavior and how they tend to react to different situations.

He as an investment advisor won't necessarily get flooded with calls from his client when he's reported, say, a $500,000 gain in the client's portfolio. But, you can bet that phone will ring off the hook when it posts a $500,000 loss! A loss always appears larger than a gain of equal size—when it goes deep into our pockets, the value of money changes.

Let's not get lost here, wealth creation and the influencers that impact our lives. Some of you may not have encountered the behavioral aspects that I am discussing currently, but you will. I want to try and explain why investors hold onto losing stocks: people often take more risks to avoid losses than to realize gains.

STOP, LET ME REPEAT THIS. (People often take more risks to avoid losses than to realize gains.)

For this reason, investors willingly remain in a risky stock position, hoping the price will bounce back. Gamblers on a losing streak will behave similarly, doubling up bets in a bid to recoup what's already been lost. So, despite our rational desire to get a return for the risks we take, we tend to value something we own higher than the price we'd normally be prepared to pay for it.

This type of loss-aversion points to another reason why investors might choose to hold their losers and sell their winners: they may believe that today's losers may soon outperform today's winners.

Investors often make the mistake of chasing market action by investing in stocks or funds which garner the most attention. Research shows that money flows into high-performance mutual funds more rapidly than money flows out from underperforming funds.

In the absence of better or new information, investors often assume that the market price is the correct price. People tend to place too much credence on recent market views, opinions, and events, and mistakenly extrapolate recent trends that differ from historical, long-term averages, and probabilities.

In bull markets, investment decisions are often influenced by price anchors, which are prices deemed significant because of their closeness to recent prices. This anchoring behavior makes the more distant returns of the past irrelevant in investors' decisions.

The question is, are you over or under-reacting? Some investors get optimistic when the market goes up, assuming it will continue to do so. Conversely, investors become extremely pessimistic during downturns. A consequence of affixing, or placing too much importance on recent events while ignoring historical data, is an over- or under-reaction to market events, which results in prices falling too much on bad news and rising too much on good news.

At the peak of optimism, investor greed moves stocks beyond their core values. When did it become a rational decision to invest in stock with zero earnings and thus an infinite price-to-earnings (P/E) ratio (think dot-com era, circa the year 2000)? Extreme cases of over- or under-reaction to market events may lead to market panics and crashes.

This is about your behavior and if it has led to overconfidence. People generally like to rate themselves as being above average in their abilities. They also overestimate the precision and veracity of their knowledge -- as well as the perceived superiority of their knowledge relative to others.

So many investors believe they can consistently time the market, but in reality, there's an overwhelming amount of evidence that proves otherwise. Overconfidence results in excess trades, with trading costs putting a dent in profits.

While much of this behavioral money matters indicates that there are also supra-individual forces at work that drive investor behavior.

For instance, individuals become far more conservative when making investment decisions on behalf of others - with people taking around one-third less risk in a portfolio intended for a child than one allocated for one's behalf. Investors even become more conservative with investments made in accounts that had culturally-salient labels such as "retirement" or "college savings."

It's understated to say that financial health affects mental and physical health and vice versa. It's just a circular thing that happens, I spoke about it in The Mindset. Consider this, when people are under stress because of finances, I heard some years ago that they release chemicals called catecholamine.

I think people have heard of things like epinephrine and stuff like that, that kind of put your whole body on fire. So that affects your mental health, affects your ability to think. It affects your physical health, wears you out, and makes you tired, you can't sleep. And then once you can't sleep, you start to have bad behaviors to deal with that."

Your Behavior

Your behavior is simply a human emotion and subjective biases when making financial decisions. What does this mean for you as an investor? By acting more or less "irrationally", you can fall victim to a series of cognitive, emotional, and social forces that lead you to make sub-optimal decisions and undermine your performance in the markets and elsewhere.

By knowing these limitations of human behavior and decision-making, people can make corrections or adjust for them. I am also implying that markets are not as efficient as standard predicts, leaving room for savvy traders to take advantage of mispricing and earn a profit.

That said, investors can be their own worst enemies. Trying to out-guess the market doesn't pay off over the long term. It often results in quirky, irrational behavior, not to mention a dent in your wealth creation. Implementing a strategy that is well thought out and sticking to it may help you avoid many of these common investing mistakes.

Chapter Six

The Circle of…

This is all about wealth creation even though the book The Mindset covered something it's important to understand that I will be mentioning your mindset. I am a very strong believer in the saying, "Strike a balance." However, I try not to dwell too much on events beyond my control.

I spoke with one of my mentors about how she knows that a stock would grow well, she replied, "I am good at what I do, but I am never sure if the stock would grow well. I can only control how I take care of them, not the outcome. I do my job well and then leave the rest to the process".

Can you recall how many hours, days, or years we spend simply focusing on and worrying about things we can't control? Just imagine how thinking positive can change your life. For you to stop feeling powerless and gain/regain control in your life, then make that decision to recognize and take advantage of what is happening in your circle of…

The circle of…? The circle of what? How many circles are there? What circles matter? Here is a list of various circles in your life, really in everyone's life at some point.

Circle of Concern
Circle of Influence
Circle of Control
Circle of Important

The Circle

Circle of Life
Circles of Purpose
Circle of Beliefs
Circle of Broke

Before I deal with all of those circles, there is one that is on the top of my mind that I wish the lesson is learned in our teen years. Being the smart person in the room imagine that being you.

I have never personally been the best at anything. Like most people (I think) I spent a lot of time growing up imagining myself as someone, I wasn't. I never pictured myself as a talk show host, an author, or even an influencer for others.

But many of you grew up with the imagination of something, the thing that you would do like sports, writing, dancing, cooking, something that you were always good/okay, but never great. Not unintelligent, but never what one would consider academic.

As you grow up into adult life, you continue a mediocrity approach (decent education, a decent job, decent books…). Never have you been bad at anything, but again you have never been great or the best.

I have to be honest here, I was very smart, but I was also bad as an abyss. So, I miss a lot of natural things that one could experience. However, I would imagine myself being somewhere like I am today other than the prison system facing me. I hoped to be the 'smartest' and 'best' in the room, in my circle, but now I appreciate how dumb those thoughts were.

What I learned through life and my journey is that being 'Smart' is Not That Smart. You know the saying they say "if you're the smartest person in the room, you're in the wrong room." I heard this quote a lot over the years, but I never really appreciated it.

It seemed like the sort of thing you say to make yourself feel better (and to justify your mediocrity). It seemed like a cop-out, but I now know it's one of the wisest mantras you can live by.

I began to realize this much later when I met people like Les Brown, George C. Fraser, Willie Gray, Tony Brown, Joe Dudley, David Bach, William Bill Cheeks, and Dale C. Bronner. I can continue with people with whom I have a personal relationship that is way smarter than me.

It didn't click into place straight away, but that's how life often goes — you hear something a lot, but it takes a while before it makes sense (before it's relevant to 'you').

So why is being so smart so dumb?

Well, I ask you to imagine what life would be like, if you entered every room knowing you were the best of the best. Would this fulfill you? Would this make you happy? Would such superiority make you complete, and better than everyone else? Or would it massage your ego into an unstoppable force?

Would it make you complacent and force you to take your eye off the ball? After all, isn't this how the likes of Blockbuster and Kodak slipped into oblivion after dominating their industry for decades?

The smartest person in the room is the only one in it incapable of learning. As the smartest person in the room, you are 'it'. What comes after 'it'… how are you supposed to motivate yourself to be better, if you're already the best or know everything?

Because if there's one thing I've learned over the last few years, it's how dangerous complacency can be. Most people make mistakes (and fail), not when they're taking a risk and pushing the boundaries, but when they sit back and relax.

Worst of all, you're blinded from the fact because you're the 'best'; you've already made it. And while you're sitting on your throne, enjoying the view, someone below you (learning from you, motivated and inspired by you) is ready to knock you off it.

Okay, okay, if we operated in our circle of influence it should represent everything we can control or affect somehow. But I feel our circle of influence is usually contained, sometimes a very small circle deep inside our circle of concern, leaving you with an area you are concerned about yet unable to alter. The only thing you could control is the effort you put into it.

In this space of wealth creation things that influence you matter, much like the mindset piece, this is all about you, not the system. However, influences come in many forms as I had listed earlier, do you know which is controlling you?

Your mindset is so influenced by the things that influence you. You must begin to identify where you should focus your time and energy. Wealth creation is a daily activity. Who's in your inner circles that is the circle of influence, and the outer circle is the Circle of Concern.

Out of all the circles I listed you should see that some should shrink and others that should expand. As an example, when your circle of influence expands, the circle of concern shrinks, and conversely, when the circle of influence shrinks, the circle of concern expands. The same is true about the circle of purpose and the circle of broke.

Focusing your energy on things you can alter can help you make more effective adjustments. It increases your circle of… and when you focus your energy on things beyond your control that circle of… shrinks.

It is a waste of time thinking about all the things that you do not have any control over. You focus your time, energy, and mental peace on such things, and you never have enough of these to focus on the positive aspects such as growth, hope, confidence, etc.

The Circle

Have you discovered that you start avoiding people who constantly talk about what's wrong in their life? People who always carry bad energy will stop coming around when your energy is placed on the things in your control.

Things that you can influence and create an impact like your saving and investing for wealth creation. These things demand your attention if you want to live a fulfilling life. Work on what you can and stop worrying about things that are not in your control.

All of this is about you. (say me, say I) You have the potential to improve your performance, personal growth, and overall enjoyment in life. Your circle of control entails how you respond to external situations. Your thoughts, your attitude, and your enthusiasm are what form your circle of control. These are the things that you have the power to control.

Here is a big secret, 'Control,' refers to what we can directly cause to happen due to our decisions, regardless of whether or not others agree. Our circle of control can only relate to ourselves in this way, and even then, only to our conscious self. What is the reason behind this? Wealth Creation

Listen, your awareness of your control and power boils to the capacity and the ability to act and perform effectively, this is the power of definition. You typically behave without conscious deliberation about how you will act and play out well-worn behavior patterns since much of what you do is habitual, or what some call "transparent".

Acting in this manner implies that you are acting outside of your immediate control. It's important to remember that habits are more than simply physical behaviors; they also encompass how you view and interpret your surroundings. Habits can be deadly.

The more your capacity for self-awareness, the greater your ability to command your state of being focusing on the Circle of . . . allows you to keep your psyche healthy. In other words, you can expect better mental wellness when your life is only focused on things that are within your control.

It becomes evident today that most of our time and energy should be focused on activities inside our sphere of influence. You will not create wealth just because, it is a life mission. You should be aware of your circle of influence and spend a reasonable amount of time there. Daily, you must engage with other individuals and communities; you must pay close attention.

None of this is just a walk in the park, there is another circle that has an impact, it's the circle of worry that should be ignored. You should strive to have no control over it. Of course, it's easier said than done. One of your biggest financial challenges will be anxiety.

This mindset isn't simply useful for dealing with anxiety. It's also a good rule to follow in many aspects of your life. What better approach to being more productive than spending less time doing things you don't have control over?

I want you to have a proactive mindset, become one of those proactive people you would want to associate with, and always scout for people with a higher Circle of Influence. But, reactive people succumb to their thoughts of negativity in response to all external events.

Proactive people stay away from people who bring negativity. It is important to understand what type of Circle of Influence you have and bring the necessary changes in outlook towards life if you want to attract all the good in life.

When you know where to look and where to concentrate, you automatically reduce your worries. In the process, you also become more productive since you stop worrying about things that are not within your control.

Increased focus is another advantage of using the circle of control. Your undivided attention remains on things that matter – things that you can control! As a result, you become more productive and effective in all aspects of life.

This is where deciding on a plan of action that you can control may be beneficial to your wealth creation. Doing something constructive, in my experience, requires you to focus on that task and breaks the cycle. It also helps you release some tension by engaging in physical activities.

The most significant advantage of worrying less is happiness. That is, at the very least, something worth pursuing. So, pause for a while and consider your options. How much time do you devote to your Circle of Influence?

Chapter Seven

Friends or Family

Now that you have thought about your circle of influencers, did you consider the impact of your friends and family? Listen, wealth creation is a combination of many various things.

When you learn what it takes, the process becomes systematic. More than anything I want to be sure that I challenged you to think about the way you think. Now, I want to talk about your friends and family and their influence on your life.

Some people may think that your family is the most important influence you have. Other people may think that friends are the most important influence. I wonder which view you agree with. Use your best examples to support your position. Yes, get paper and pen and write it down now for the record.

Would you believe that we are all influenced by whomever we may meet? We all stand as models to everyone in this world.

However, your choice of a model is important, especially when choosing your path to wealth creation. I believe that in the case concerning your future and maybe your career family could have more influence on you than friends.

Friend or Family

Your friends are the ones you spend time having fun, enjoying, playing, and so forth. Your friends also may teach you good things and help you from time to time. Your friends will advise good things about life, but not like your family.

Your family is always thinking that their bloodline will become superior ones in the future. They want their bloodline to be smarter than anyone else. However, friends are not such influential advisers as your family.

Your family often feels that time is wasted when you are having too much fun. But, your friends influence you more to play or have fun rather than advising you about your future.

Therefore, the family uses their influence to impact your future. I believe that most people are usually influenced by their friends rather than their family. It depends on what type of influence it is.

Family members choose their future. What they see around them influences them. However, this influence might not be good for their future.

Let me say this, regardless of what you think about my thoughts about "WHO" it is that is influencing you, there is a set of facts that I want you to consider. What legacy of generational wealth are you being influenced by from your family and your friends?

Don't get me wrong I believe that friends and family are the true cause of happiness. When you have friends and family, you have those who care for you. When you have them, you don't need anything else (my opinion). When you have a family and some really good friends, you know that they will always be there for you.

You know that you can always count on them, and you know that you can trust them with a secret or anything personal. When you are surrounded by them, you realize that nothing in the world can ever replace them. Am I pouring it on?

Nothing can ever replace the memories that you have. No matter how much money, how famous, or how glamorous you are, it wouldn't be that great if you didn't have friends or a family. I would never trade them for anything.

I would like to be rich, have pretty shoes, expensive purses, own a ton of make-up, and have a whole closet full of clothes. But my family and my friends are much more important. They don't even care about what I look like or what I wear. I could wake up looking like a freak, and it wouldn't matter.

They don't care about looks. And, they don't care that I'm NOT perfect. I don't have to put on an act like I'm all that just to hang out with them. I could act like a total loser and dress up like a crown at the mall and they would start laughing.

People would be looking at us like we are crazy. But we would just laugh knowing that we look retarded. They wouldn't say, "I don't know her" or something like that. Okay, maybe they would, but that is the fun part.

Friend or Family

If you have only money, you will be lonely and the only thing you can do is buy things that don't have any value if you have no one to share them with. Being lonely in a huge house and with lots of stuff just lying around might be great for show and all, but when it comes to things that truly matter, friends and family, are what's really important.

If I were rich, I would like that at first, but then it would get annoying. Not knowing who your friends are or not knowing who is using you and who is really there for you. Then, having some friends only because I am as rich as you are. I'm not saying you don't need money, because everybody needs some. But it's not the most important thing.

I do not know if any of that resonated with you, I was speaking of the many ways that one can be influenced and misguided about wealth and wealth creation. It makes it sounds as if money is just a thing, not that important.

So I decided that I wanted to do a little research on friends and family among some clients and friends. What I wanted was an honest answer to these questions and their opinions. My first case was a lady in her mid-thirties who was very eager to talk about the influences of a friend.

“Friends are the biggest value in people’s lives. I have many friends. Most of them are my neighbors, but also I have friends in my business world. I can go out somewhere with them and feel comfortable. I know that my friends will help me through anything. I can trust them. I have one best friend. I may say I admire his faith. Our friendship can be firm and intense. He always helps me get through tough times and treats me with respect.

As a friend of mine, he has never lied to me. If I am upset, my best friend will do all he can to cheer me up. He is caring, cheerful, trustworthy, outgoing, and good-tempered. He is younger than I am. I think that age is not important for a friendship if you can come to an understanding and respect each other.

I have friends among people of many different generations. I like friends a little younger because I can be childish sometimes. Older people in my life are serious and calm. They care about their immediate and future to some degree. They have less free time.

However, I like them because they teach me things and share their experience. Older friends also may help me to navigate life and explain to me what I cannot understand.

Friends are one of life's treasures so we have to treasure our friendships. It is not easy to make friends nowadays. A true friend should be honest and trustworthy. Without these characteristics, you cannot have a friendship with value. People must be sociable, tolerant, conscientious, and good-tempered if they want to make friends.

Furthermore, they must understand the other person's feelings and moods and always help them. If people want not to lose old friends, they should care about them. They should call them and ask how they are.

I suppose that friendship is a state in which you feel important and you know that you can do something helpful for your friend. Sometimes you see somebody for the first time and you feel you have been friends for years.

I deliberated hard about using this story, then I realized that this is bigger than me. Nothing in her entire story talked about wealth, finances, or personal growth. This is such a common approach with so many people. You are going to have to be a part of the 3% of wealth creators or settle.

I want you to relate as much information as possible. I do not just want you to be a reader only, in fact, I am trying to influence you as much as I can. You may not realize it but you probably let people around you influence your spending from time to time. It's nearly impossible to avoid letting people influence your spending all of the time, and sometimes it can even be a good thing.

During my finance journey over the past few years, I've realized that the people you surround yourself with can have a big impact on your financial goals positively or negatively.

Unfortunately, most of the time when friends and family influence your spending it's not a good thing.

They may convince you to spend money on drinks, dinner, and a night out even though you know you shouldn't. Do they convince you? Otherwise. Bye, bye budget! Bye, bye wealth creation.

If you want to make progress on your financial goals this year, you need to stop letting friends and family influence your spending. Here are some ways your family and friends influence your spending and how you can stop it from happening. Maybe…

Do not fall under peer pressure at all. It amazes me when I see a 45 years old person being led by someone in their thirties on a decision that sets them back in a financial situation.

Listen closely, do your peers give you the best influence or the worst influence? When it comes to finances there is some positive peer pressure. You know you should have an IRA or 401(k).

You know you should save more than you spend, and you know you should pay off your credit card right away. This is all positive peer pressure to help you become better with your finances. Question? You do know, right?

Negative peer pressure is when they help talk you into buying something that you know is out of your budget, even if it is on sale. You may have hesitations, but you buy it anyway. Because you just need to show them.

The best way to avoid this is to simply stay away from negative peer pressure. Find friends that lift you up and support your goals. But if you really can't avoid some of these people, try to keep your receipts so you can return items later. They'll never know! (Except the one that pushed you to buy for them.)

Again, this can be both bad and good. If Mom and Dad gave to charity, saved, and lived well below their means good for them and good for you from learning those habits.

But, if Mom and Dad took out credit card after credit card and never paid in full, learning from them is not so great. For better or worse, our parents are usually the first financial influencer we will have. Just keep in mind that you don't have to do everything they did.

Ah, jealousy rears its ugly head. This is one of the biggest drivers of overspending. A friend or family member might have just bought a new house, new car, or cool new gadget. This often leads you to wonder how come you don't have a house, car, or gadget just as cool (if not cooler) than theirs.

You are not alone in thinking this. These thoughts go through almost everyone's mind at some point. That jealousy will often lead you to buy something to keep up, even if you can't afford it.

Instead of going shopping and trying to keep up out of jealousy, do your best to remember why you are living on a budget. Most likely you have some kind of reward to look forward to, so try to keep that in mind too. Best of all, remember to be grateful for the things you do have already.

Expectations, especially from family members, are the worse and sometimes can quickly get out of hand. Family, friends, and even society expect you to get a "good" job, buy a large house, have a fancy car, etc. If this is what is expected of you, you might incur large debt just to save face and appear as successful as they want you to be. Don't fall for it! Stay true to yourself, your budget, and your priorities.

Shaming is hurtful and it comes in more forms than you think. Shaming can go both ways. Shame on you for being poor and getting food stamps. Or, shame on you for flaunting the wealth you worked for while people are starving in other countries.

Shaming often leads to guilt, which is a huge proponent of spending. You may feel guilty about earning more than friends or family and end up spending money on them to make yourself feel better.

Just remember, everyone's situation is different. Don't give into shame, and especially don't go shaming others.

Most important of all is to remember that not everyone is out to make you get off track with your financial goals and influence you to spend your money. They may not know they are causing you to get off track with your goals if you've never told them. But if they do know about your goals, you might want to rethink how often you meet up with them. The easiest way to avoid letting others negatively influence our spending is to avoid it altogether.

Like I said wealth creation is a combination of many various things, a little of this and a little of that. Sometimes, it even needs a sprinkle of this too and that too. Be it, a friend or family.

Chapter Eight

Your Money

You would think that money itself would be an influencer, but it is not. There are so many books and tapes on "how to gain more money," "how to attract money," and other aspects of how money works are relevant to your progress, understanding the philosophical nature of money is vital for wise use of wealth creation.

In this chapter, I will try to break down the reasons you should view money as an influencer rather than an end goal by itself. I want you to explore positive and negative money mindsets, seeking to build a healthy relationship with your money.

Without money, affording basic needs like food, shelter, and clothing would be impossible. Therefore, we use money to be able to sustain our lives at the very least. Of course, you could resort to the good old barter trade, giving out your labor and certain assets you have in exchange for the most important things you need.

But the truth is, few people accept barter trade and so it'll be an inefficient way to sustain life. However, everyone recognizes money as having value to help them acquire their necessities so they'll be ready to take it from you to give you what you need.

Recently as I was writing "The Mindset" I spoke with Nathaniel Bronner Jr. about a quote for the book. In our discussion, he shared with me how he has revamped the way he measures his time, his very words to me were "Time is money". It is also a term people use to defend their time. In some ways, this is true. When we reverse this statement, we can say that money avails our time.

Think about it — if you'd like to visit your family during the weekend but also have to fix your leaking faucet, you may have to postpone the visit so that you may fix it. But if you have money to hire a plumber, you can hire them and spend that time visiting your family.

I know that I rather delegate many things to a professional than spend time dealing with them myself. This is a luxury money can afford. So in this case, you can see money as an influencer that also buys you time to work on more fulfilling priorities.

Listen it can be difficult to learn to manage money. However, if you ever want to transition from simply "having money" to "wealthy," you need to understand the importance of money management and begin implementing it regarding your finances.

There are so many who make a decent amount of money but aren't practicing money management and tend to simply spend money without any rhyme, reason, or purpose. Money comes in and it goes out, while the person remains stagnant and doesn't ever move forward. Little influence.

On the other hand, those who have wealth, tend to have peace of mind. They aren't looking for money or things for fulfillment, yet they know that they have all that they need and will continue to throughout their life. Oh my, let me say that again, no you read it again. Big influence.

To embrace money management is to learn financial practices that will help you accumulate wealth and create it while understanding the key to preserving that wealth. Implementing the management of your money takes your unique needs, goals, and risks into consideration while focusing on your financial decision-making and your previous habits that could stand in the way of your success.

It also includes a humble awareness of certain factors outside of your control, such as inflation, taxes, debt, and market volatility. This is it, right here, I struggle with my thoughts trying to get it all out.

Learning the basic code of belief of money management will help you to understand why it's important and how to start implementing the practice for yourself as your influencer. Not understanding the foundation of money creates a multitude of issues.

For example, if you aren't aware of the way credit and interest work, you might charge something small on a credit card that ends up costing you 20 percent or more in interest over a year. You could end up paying for that one thing over and over again, essentially throwing your money away, and making it difficult to achieve wealth creation.

I want you to have a firm, educated grasp of financial matters, so you will not end up like the majority of Americans; locked into years of debt, paying high fees, and unsure where all of your money is going. This is a killer to wealth creation.

When you understand money management and utilize principles to secure your financial wealth, you can eliminate debt-inducing mistakes that leave you bound to creditors and even to material goods. Along those lines, a good skill to learn regarding money management is how to control your decision, which will help you gain financial independence as you build wealth.

As you embrace financial money management and begin to create goals you get to the bottom line in everything you need to know and where you're headed. Without a clear destination, (wealth creation) you're more than likely going to keep going around in circles.

Your Wealth Creation GPS isn't programmed, your map's not out, and you are not driving in one set direction. Instead, you're just driving. That's exactly what it's like to be dealing with money without goals. You are wracking in an income every month and you are just throwing that money around with reckless abandon because you have no set purpose.

However, if you establish your financial goals, you're going to have something programmed into your Wealth Creation GPS. You will know exactly where you're headed and what you want to do with that money. You will be prepared to intentionally use or save every dollar that comes your way and start wealth creation.

By setting your big goals, you'll also be able to set some smaller goals that act as steps along the way. These small goals are milestones that help you to progress further down the path to your financial destination.

These small goals are the little pit stops along the way. While the rest area, the gas station, and the park may not be the place you want to stay, they help rejuvenate you and give you a boost of energy to set back out again.

Your goals are also useful for showing you things to avoid. If something is way out of the way or you'll even have to backtrack to go there, it's not a step you're going to want to take. Your goals will give you clarity and vision, helping you make the best decisions for reaching them.

Money management and wealth are all about accumulation. Many people don't understand this. They view wealth as making a lot of money and don't realize that if they're spending that money, no matter how much it is, and not accumulating it, they're never going to be wealthy. I tell my clients and students that it is all about accumulation, not liquidation.

This is why you need to determine where your money is going. When you can see where your money is going, you will then be able to develop a strategic plan for using, saving, and investing it more effectively.

The Money

Businesses understand the importance of money management in business and focus on increasing their monthly profits. However, increasing profit isn't the end goal. Using the increased profit wisely to further financial growth is essential.

Thus, creating a money management plan that includes an investment of the additional profit will increase the wealth of the business exponentially. Whether you are managing money for yourself or a business, the stronger your money management plan, and the more control you have over the flow of your cash, the closer you are to reaching your goals of wealth creation

Money as your influencer requires you to have a long-term investment strategy. It is the key to strong and effective money management and wealth accumulation. When you create a long-term strategy, you're more likely to keep your eyes on the prize and not be swayed by the many things that come your way.

There are numerous fads and wealth-building ideas out there that don't have a foundation or a proven reputation. However, they sound great, causing many financially undisciplined people to jump on the bandwagon, wasting time and a whole lot of money. DO NOT DO THAT

An investment strategy helps YOU stay focused, moving towards your small milestones instead of veering off in every which way. You are better able to ignore the stepping stones that others are putting in your path to keep on heading in the right direction towards your own goals.

Poor management of risk is one of the main causes of investment underperformance. You need to be proactive when it comes to risk management, understanding the risk-return relationship, and acting on it. Being deliberate with risk serves to drive return performance and achieve both short-term and long-term results.

When you have a seamless money management plan, you will understand the market risks and the likelihood of negative returns. You will be cognizant of the fact that holding your portfolio longer means more negative returns in some cases, yet also means a greater probability of a positive annual return.

Understanding your taxes is a huge part of money management. While everyone knows that they pay taxes, they're not aware of how much they pay. They certainly don't know about unnecessary taxes and how they can hinder the accumulation of wealth.

When you are managing your money, you aren't thinking of your income as everything you make. Instead, you know that your income is really whatever you make after taxes, enabling you to better allocate your finances.

In regards to investments, you will want to consider your account location, essentially allocating your money based on your tax status. You will then do the same for your various investments, allocating them in the same manner.

This will give you a better understanding of your overall wealth, and your options for wealth distribution, and will help you accumulate wealth faster. If you read the mindset you already know.

When you begin to accumulate wealth, you're opening yourself up to a variety of areas of risk. One vulnerability can destroy your wealth and everything you have worked for. The greater wealth you have, the greater risks you'll have. When your purchases are larger and more expensive, you experience the potential for risk along with each purchase. Do not get comfortable.

You are putting yourself out there with everything you buy, every trip you take, and everything new you try. Every time you use your wealth, you are exposing your finances and dancing around risk. Unfortunately, every risk can bring it all down. Please remember this.

Awareness of the great risks involved with having wealth can help you create a money management plan that seeks to avoid them. A risk management assessment can help you uncover your potential risks and mitigate them.

As you create your plan, consider circumstances such as:

- An accident or illness that causes long-term income loss.
- An unexpected, early death of the income provider.
- Property damage and medical needs.
- Liability claims which expose assets.
- Financial exposure from domestic staff.
- Identity theft or fraud.
- Loss of business.

With awareness of the potential of these and other circumstances, you will be better able to create a money management plan that is prepared for these issues. Preparation can help you avoid great, and even total, loss. Your money is an influencer.

When you accumulate wealth, you will be able to increase your capital, create security for your family, make positive investments, better your standard of living, and develop a cushion in the form of assets and savings. Overall, money management increases your lifestyle, providing security and greater opportunity for you and your family.

Even though you know money as an influencer do not fall for ads that promise you more money to motivate you to buy. The frequency of the usage of money as a motivational tool in our culture has greatly damaged the way people view money. So many spend money to satisfy their ego since more money can give them more power and status.

Some view money as a source of happiness as they see people flaunting their "happiness" in the things that cost more money than the middle class can afford. But the replacement of self-worth with money never works. It's a rat race. And if you're honest with yourself, you can see it in people's lives around you and maybe in your own.

And the truth is, the moment you strive to get more money so others can like you, money ceases to be an influencer and you become its tool. Instead of it working for you, you start working for it. You get lost in money while you move along in life, ignoring your real purposes. And if you think of it, when will "getting more money" as a goal end?

Would you be satisfied when you get the virtually unlimited supply of money circulating all over the world or would you have to stop when you die since getting all the money in the world is impossible?

It's time to pause and figure out the things you value if you'd care less what anyone thinks of you. See how you can attain that with the most minimum of resources and continue attaining wealth whenever you have an opportunity.

Chapter Nine

Next Generational

If you didn't need to worry about money ever again, would your life be any different than it is today? For most of us, the answer is a resounding yes. Generational wealth is important because money holds most people back from living the life they truly desire.

There are many ways generational wealth will change your life and the life of those you love. Wealth creation creates the opportunity for you to safeguard your independence, provide for those you love, establish a legacy and have the freedom to live a life of your choosing. The goal is to ensure you and your future generations never need to worry about money again.

Understanding why generational wealth should be an influencer starts with understanding why wealth is important. Wealth is an accumulation of a significant amount of money, valuable possessions, property, and other riches. Generational wealth adds to the concept of wealth that you are also focusing on ways to preserve and transfer the wealth you created.

A good way to look at wealth is from the perspective that everything on this earth is yours for but a time. You are a steward of the riches of the earth, but you cannot take your wealth with you. It is part of the beauty of life in many ways.

You have a time on this earth and when that time is gone, it's gone. Everything you do while you are on earth is a part of your legacy. The same holds true for your wealth. For many, never needing to worry about money again allows you to focus on the things that truly matter in life.

Earlier in this book, I referenced that as a child, you grow up following your parents' rules. You know as long as you live under their roof, you will be subject to their rules. As you grow up, you begin to dream about what it would be like to make your own rules.

If you have a curfew, you imagine getting to stay out as long as you want. If your parents forced you to eat vegetables or limited your screen time each day, you dreamed of eating what you want and playing when you want.

You couldn't wait until you were out on your own, so you could make your own rules. As an adult, you learned that freedom was more elusive than you first thought it has a cost.

When you started working, you realized your supervisor could decide when you came into work and what things you worked on when you were there. They could determine if you received a raise and whether you were promoted. Even professional athletes quickly realized they had to abide by the rules set by their coach and their organization.

Regardless of the situation, you will notice if you are dependent on another person in some way, you will need to consider their wishes. In fact, the more dependent you are, the more consideration you need to give to their opinions. In the relationship with your parents, you knew as long as they were feeding you, paying your bills, and providing shelter for you, you needed to follow their rules.

At work, as long as you were receiving a check from your organization, they would have a say in some part of your life. As much as you wanted your independence, you realized having to follow the instructions of another person is not always a bad thing. Oftentimes, your parents were right and you needed to eat your vegetables. Early in your career, listening to your more experienced supervisor was a good thing.

As a professional athlete, when you are early in your career, the organization may have a better idea about how to build a winning organization and culture. This is a good reminder that even though you may have secured independence for your future generations, it doesn't mean you don't need guidance.

You don't want to give them the independence to make decisions when they have no established values or understanding. Generational wealth is important because when most people realize what they want in life, they have financial constraints that hinder their ability to pursue their purpose.

These are some and there are more reasons to discuss why generational wealth is important. Of all the reasons you have read so far, the freedom to live the life of your choosing is what you are striving for. The reason is, that when you start living a life of your choosing, you stop worrying about money. We all have worried about money at some point in our lives.

Some worry about money day to day, while others worry about money when they have large purchases. Some feel comfortable about money today and worry about money in the future. Whether that future is your retirement or your future generations you can worry about money whether you have a lot or a little.

You have to develop major confidence in the process and have patience with yourself. The notion that having a lot of money means you don't worry about money is not true.

Those who don't worry about money have a plan to address their goals and fears. If you have ever seen someone walk on a tightrope, you are amazed by their ability to perform without a fear of falling.

While it does seem like an amazing feat for you or I do, the performer thinks nothing of it. The difference has little to do with your appetite for risk versus theirs. The difference is they have practiced walking a tightrope. The performer has fallen a few times, but ultimately learned a strategy that will effectively ensure they don't fall.

Since you have never walked a tightrope, you don't have a plan to ensure you can successfully make it across. That is why those who have walked a tightrope for many decades will walk a tightrope across the Empire State building or the Grand Canyon. They are not crazy; they just have confidence in the process and know the result they will achieve.

For you to never worry about money again, you need a comprehensive plan that addresses each of your financial concerns. The plan should take your present and future goals into consideration. You should be provided with a framework that has you as confident in your abilities to perform as the person who is willing to walk a tightrope across the Grand Canyon.

I think that I was digressing back to money, let me get back to generational wealth creation. All of this is a big bowl of soup with a lot of awesome ingredients.

This has got to be what you were waiting for. I would not be surprised if you have just skipped through the book to get to this part. If you did you may end up disappointed. You see I intentionally place key parts of this chapter in every other chapter to hinder skipping around.

Generational wealth—sometimes referred to as legacy wealth or family wealth—is financial assets that are passed down from one generation to the next. For example, from you to your children, to their children, and so on. Generational wealth can include real estate property, money, investments, stocks, bonds, family businesses, or anything that has a monetary value.

Wealth creation is not about budgeting, debt, credit, leveraging, and credit scores. Wealth creation is about wealth transfer and should be an influencer. The term general wealth transfer simply refers to the act of transferring generational wealth (i.e. money, property, etc.) to your children or grandchildren. With proper generational wealth planning and management, wealth can be passed down for many generations within your family.

Generational Wealth

This form of Generational wealth is important because it can offer a significant financial advantage to your family. For example, if your children or grandchildren received a financial advantage early on in their life, this could help them pay for their university or college education alleviating the need for the student loan debt, or be used for a down payment on a home. This creates a significant advantage for young adults starting their life in the real world.

People have always asked me how much money is considered generational wealth? For any amount of wealth to be considered generational wealth, it simply has to be passed down by at least one generation; however, there is no definitive number that constitutes generational wealth because wealth is relative. The amount of passed-down family wealth all depends on the recipients and how it is used.

For example, if you received $1 million dollars in generational wealth but only need $250,000 to live comfortably for the remainder of your life, the million would be more than enough to be considered generational wealth and could continue to be passed down to your future generations. On the other hand, if you inherited $1 million dollars but spent it all within your lifetime, the money would not go further than one generation.

I have clients asking should they fear their children will not have anything to pass down to their children. Reasons for their concern include high cost of living, lack of financial knowledge, splurging, and losing their inheritance due to divorce.

Building generational wealth that can be passed down from generation to generation requires a large amount of wealth, strategic financial and estate planning, as well as financially responsible spending by those who inherit it.

You can accumulate generational wealth by acquiring assets, investing in assets that produce wealth, or simply by saving money that you don't intend to spend during your retirement, to pass it down to your future generations.

There are many ways to build generational wealth. I have to go back and say a few things I believe are important. Think back to your younger years. If you drowned in student debt or never knew what it meant to save money, you likely suffered.

You had to figure out how to make ends meet, let alone find a way to save. You cannot turn back the clock, but you can teach your children starting now how to manage money and start investing.

Generational wealth creation is money you pass down to them and future generations. Knowing that you've created a healthy financial future for your loved ones is something most people only dream of, but don't know how to achieve.

You are no different from most people you put generational wealth out of your mind because you have more pressing matters. Current financial needs, debts, emergency savings, and retirement often supersede saving for future generations. Fortunately saving for future generations is easy when you manage your financial plan right and the guidance that I am creating.

Everyone, yes I said everyone can provide generational wealth and not just in cold, hard cash. Stocks, real estate properties, and other assets provide just as much value, if not more. It starts with one step. Take the plunge, set the intention, and you will pave the way to long-term financial success for you and your loved ones.

Chapter Ten

Building Your Legacy

You can't leave your family money when you are in debt. Create a debt payoff strategy (www.budgetaction.com) and consistently pay your debt down or off completely. Check out the debt payoff platform to help you get started on your debt-free strategy today.

Always save for retirement. Retirement planning is crucial to building family wealth. If your employer offers a 401K, use it, especially if they match your contributions. If your employer doesn't offer retirement plans or you have more money you can save for retirement, open an IRA, Roth IRA, or taxable investment account.

Once you get yourself out of debt, stock your emergency fund, create a retirement plan, and reach financial freedom, you can focus on building your generational wealth.

Creating generational wealth doesn't happen overnight. It doesn't happen in a few months either. Building wealth is a lifelong process that starts with these steps. Building generational wealth starts with a plan or a foundation. If you aren't financially secure, you won't be able to leave behind a legacy.

Assess your financial situation today. Pull out your bank statements, investment statements, and credit card statements.

Take stock of your assets and liabilities. Look at your budget too. If you don't have one, create one now.

Generational wealth is important because it is about more than just passing on your wealth. Generational wealth is about passing on your values through your wealth to future generations. You want to share the wisdom you have learned along the way that has led to your success.

You can be as smart as anything you want to describe, it does not matter when it comes to wealth creation. It is the wisdom that you discover along the way that becomes your most valuable asset to transfer to the next generation.

This is not only key to ensuring your future generations don't lose their wealth, it is important to safeguard your future generations' work ethic and self-image. Generational wealth is your way to show your family why family is worth investing in and what skills you think will help them succeed.

Do you want to emphasize education or do you want to shine a light on entrepreneurship? Is it important for your family to volunteer and give back to the community or do you want to make sure they invest in real estate?

All of this leads you to keep in mind that whatever riches you accumulate on earth are yours but for a short while, you want to create something that represents your values. Your legacy can be represented in many ways. Some will use their wealth to create a foundation or nonprofit that will fight for a cause they believe in.

For example, the Bill and Melinda Gates foundation focuses on providing clean water to communities that have none.

Growing up in a single-parent household, Warrick Dunn's foundation focuses on building homes for single mothers in need. Others will choose to use their wealth to build a legacy within their family.

If education is important to you, then you can set aside funds to pay for your children's or grandchildren's college education. With a large enough fund, you can create a trust to pay for the college education of multiple generations.

Other families believe starting a business should be prioritized over formal education. They want to pass on a legacy of entrepreneurship, problem-solving, and helping others. This is commonly the case with a family who has built their wealth from a business.

They want their children involved in the business and knowledgeable enough to start their own or take over the family business. To effectively pass on an entrepreneur's legacy, you need to set some ground rules. You need to consider matters regarding the type of business you would be willing to fund.

Is there a list of industries that would be acceptable? Would any business have an opportunity to be funded? Does the approval process require a business plan or will you establish a mini-board of senior family members who have approval authority?

These are all things you need to consider when building a legacy. If there is a friend, school, nonprofit, or religious organization you have been supporting while alive, what happens when you're gone? It is worth considering if you would like to make a one-time donation in your will or whether you would like to allocate funds for perpetuity.

We haven't even started discussing what you want to do with your physical assets. Is land ownership important to you? If it is, decide what you want to do to make sure your children are not selling your land for cash.

Investing in real estate is a common way to create generational wealth. This can include a single investment property or multiple investment properties. Your real estate portfolio can be used to build your estate plan when deciding how to distribute your wealth to future generations.

And although real estate values can fluctuate from time to time due to the market, it is still one of the best methods to build and maintain generational wealth.

I know you have known this all of your life. So, why haven't you started buying and owning as many homes as possible? Oh, oh, why are you still renting? No, Let me put this another way, why are you still paying someone else mortgage? If you are dead bent on paying someone else mortgage please email as soon as possible.

I will come back to this again, you have so many influencers in this space. Consider saving money is one of the simplest ways to generate wealth. By moving money into a savings account and setting it aside for the next generation, the money will be designated for that purpose and carried out with that intention.

Be mindful, however, that putting money away into a savings account does not guarantee the greatest return. Inflation will always play a role in determining generational wealth as well; the value of $1 today will not be the same in five years. That's why it is important to always ensure your savings are generating high interest to secure your family's financial future.

You created your financial foundation. Now it's time to get down to the nitty-gritty – setting up your generational wealth. The stock market is a great place to start and begin the diversification of your assets.

Many people assume only the wealthy can invest in the stock market, but today it's easier than ever. Beginners looking to dip their toe in without getting overwhelmed love platforms like Acorn and Betterment.

You don't need a minimum amount invested, so start with $5 if that's what it takes. You can also speak with an investment advisor if you are not sure where to start.

Make sure any money you invest in the stock market you leave long enough to create earnings. You want the compound earnings. Think of it as a long-term investment strategy. Invest a few thousand dollars today and leave it for 30 years and leave a nice nest egg for your family

Stock market investments such as index funds are a fanatic way to generate passive income to protect long-term wealth from inflation. A mutual fund or exchange-traded fund (ETF) are perfect examples of investment funds within the stock market that can build generational wealth that can be passed down to your family members.

Building generational wealth isn't about getting lucky or beating the stock market. Here are five strategies for growing your net worth and ensuring you have assets to pass down through the generations.

Generational wealth is growing, it's considered a concept that more and more individuals and families are thinking about. The largest wealth transfer in history is taking place right now, I was reading somewhere that an estimated $30 trillion is being passed on from Baby Boomers to their children. Plus, the tech and crypto boom has helped many in their 30s and 40s explore this concept.

While this is no question a big part of what comprises generational wealth, there's another much more complex side to the topic: making sure your heirs do things like use their money wisely and can live a fulfilling life, and ensuring that future generations can continue to benefit from the wealth you're building today.

Many of today's millionaires are first-generation and you will likely be also. In my book The Mindset, we looked at the most realistic ways to build a substantial portfolio in your lifetime, focusing on the core idea of increasing wealth.

Ideally, you're able to take advantage of compound interest for as long as possible. After all, while Warren Buffet has a great track record of picking investments, his overall success is largely because he's been steadily investing over a 70-year time horizon.

While real estate — including homeownership and real estate entrepreneurship — are touted as the best ways to build wealth, research shows that the majority of today's millionaires got rich from investment appreciation, employee compensation, and stock options/profit sharing. To me, what these things have in common is that they require a long-term commitment.

A million-dollar portfolio only comes after decades of staying in the market. Highly-paid employees can bring the most value to an organization, which comes from taking the time to develop high-value skills.

As much as I love entrepreneurship, building a company that's going to last decades and allow you to continuously have a large gap between your income and expenses for decades is hard. And with real estate, since leverage is used, all it takes is one market crash over your lifetime to wipe you out.

If you're looking to create generational wealth — whether you're someone who has already accumulated the assets or someone who wants to put themselves on the right trajectory — here are some more strategies to consider.

A family money mission statement is a document that gives family members, including yourself, a clear sense of purpose and values when it comes to money.

The idea of a family money mission statement is similar to why a business goes about creating its mission statement: it's not about the tactical strategies, but about the principles and values that you want to carry through the generations.

If you want to enjoy enduring success have a core purpose and core values that remain fixed while your strategies and practices endlessly adapt to a changing world.

The rare ability to balance continuity and change–requiring a consciously practiced discipline–is closely linked to the ability to develop a vision. Vision guides what to preserve and what to change. I preach this all the time, I hope it is received by you.

If you have already started accumulating wealth over your lifetime — and I can't emphasize this enough — your heirs should be a part of the process of creating a family money mission statement!

It's your heirs that are going to be the ones seeing out the mission and vision of your document. You want them as involved as possible. If you're in the early stages of your life, this process is beneficial for helping you make career and investment decisions over the decades to come.

You show know by now that a different mindset and strategy are needed when you're looking to invest in a way that's going to be sustainable for multiple generations. Your goal becomes not only to have enough money to last throughout your lifetime but also to maximize and preserve your assets for future generations.

If you have the risk tolerance to stomach the wild swings in the crypto market, that's great. But there's no guarantee your heirs will, and when prices hit an all-time low, they may sell at the absolute worst possible time.

We're often taught to think of the power of compound interest in short time frames, such as 10 or 20 years. But when we can extend our timeline to 50 or 60 years, we get very interesting results that are hard for us to comprehend — like turning $1 million into $34 million.

When you're dealing with long-term time horizons, a massive sum of money isn't needed upfront to create wealth for future generations. You need to invest in a way that allows you to stay in the market for decades.

Over your lifetime, as well as the lifetime of your heirs, assets in your estate will need to be sold. Whether it's to pay debts, to pay taxes, or even to provide payments to your heirs, these events, as much as possible, need to be planned for ahead of time. When estates don't plan for liquidity, they often have to sell more illiquid assets, like real estate or business interests, at an inopportune time.

Your Legacy

Changing the speed of wealth creation is the core of my belief. When I think about building a legacy I have my mind set on business wealth creation. Realizing that so many people think of business revenue as income month to month, it's not. It should be the building process of your legacy.

Having securities or ownership of a family business can be included in generational wealth. Where there is a successful business to pass down there are often financial and career advantages.

Family businesses offer a means of ongoing income, revenue, and money as well as career opportunities that would not otherwise be available to someone outside of the family.

Life insurance can help you pass down wealth for your family and maximize the amount of wealth that is passed down. There are several tax advantages to having life insurance since no estate taxes are owed on life insurance and life insurance policies are not counted as part of an estate and therefore are not taxed by the federal government.

The benefits of life insurance are that there is more money to pass down to your heirs and it minimizes your estate taxes. Life insurance can also help provide financial support for dependents in the event of an untimely death.

Did you know that 68% of affluent families have not discussed instructions for their estate with their heirs? To distribute any accumulated generational wealth, this will need to be determined as part of your estate planning. To pass down generational wealth, you will need a legal will, a trust, and named beneficiaries.

Of the many reasons you should have a will, having full control over the wealth you leave your family for generations to come is one of the most important. People WHO have a will have made or updated their will/end-of-life plans.

While finalizing the details of your last will and testament, a trust fund (or trust funds) should be set up as part of your estate planning. Assets placed within a trust avoid probate and certain taxes, further maximizing the wealth passed down to the named beneficiaries within your family.

Once you have generated enough wealth to secure your family's financial future, you must include the details of this wealth within a will to ensure it is properly handled and distributed.

There is a stage of wealth creation that is called the wealth preservation stage. Some people are calling this stage the wealth distribution stage. The rationale is that you are distributing wealth to yourself. But the name does not matter. It is the stage where you live from your investments.

During this stage, you want to preserve your wealth. You want your wealth to last as long as possible because you will live from your wealth. At this stage, you want to make sure that your withdrawal strategy is sound. You want to know what you will sell and when you will sell it to live from your investments. If you only have cash, you may not need such a strategy. But cash will not sustain you long enough.

See you may need to be less aggressive. Most people will switch a part of their portfolio to bonds at this stage. It is not mandatory to do so, but it could be good for your peace of mind.

Another way to prepare for this stage is to start accumulating a larger buffer of cash. For me, I would prepare a one-year buffer before I would retire. This would help not to have to sell at the wrong time.

Finally, if you plan on retiring with a house and no income, you may have to consider paying off your mortgage (or reducing it) before this stage. Without any income, you may not qualify to renew a mortgage after your retirement. And the bank may force you to sell your house. It is important to consider that in the transition between the accumulation and preservation stage.

Chapter Eleven

My Final Words

If I would have targeted individuals who are considered to be finance influencers, you would not have looked deep inside of yourself for what you allow to influence you. There is a new breed of influencers taking the social media world by storm. The world of finance used to be the realm of old, white-haired men doling out advice about cutting back on five-dollar coffee and saving up.

These days, up-and-coming finance influencers are younger than ever. And they're introducing personal finance management to a new audience who are craving to learn how to handle their finances better. This may include you as well. That is not enough, only you can discover that drive that is inside of you.

Back in the day, if people wanted to figure out which stocks to invest in, they would consult finance authorities like the Wall Street Journal for investment advice. Today, though, these sources are often seen as outdated and even boring. Most cannot relate to the information these platforms provide especially since they're not designed for beginner investors.

The younger generations also feel unrepresented since these institutions target an older, wealthier class of audience instead of Gen Zers and Millennials who are learning to invest for the first time at such an early age. When I sit down with this audience they seem more prepared to set new principles and foundations. Frankly,

I do not like it at all, I love it!

See, this is where social media and influencers come into play. Both have transformed the way people consume information and act upon it. Influencers focusing on financial advice now provide bite-sized personal finance information to an audience hungry for knowledge and guidance. Be very careful in this process, I say stay hungry, not thirsty.

What makes these finance influencers important in some way? In today's culture as they discuss topics relevant to their audience—from how to pay off student loans or save up money to buy a house by the age of 30 to how to get rid of credit card debt or start investing in the stock market. It's this relevancy that makes them effective and popular among the younger crowd.

Another key aspect is they come with different specialties and target specific demographics. There are finance influencers who focus on investing and those who put an emphasis on personal finance and creating generational wealth. Others choose to discuss topics like wealth building and eliminating debt, whose audiences include couples and women of color.

All of this is significant in many ways, my main mission is for you to first improve and change the conversations you have around money by learning from others' experiences. If you are highly active on your socials, you will discover many offering advice on money and sharing insights.

I believe that I have been putting out savvy advice about budgeting discussing where to save and when to splurge on purchases, and inspiring and actionable advice about personal finance, self-care, and life in general.

I want to be clear on how you should find investing accessible for you and anyone who might not typically invest. It is so important to invest, build wealth, and manage money. Many of you have experienced the struggle of figuring your way out of your debts and likewise want to boost your investment knowledge by understanding the stock market.

But, if I am successful with creating an engagement with you that express interest and enjoyment, you can process deeply and pay attention, and continue in these efforts as if time and the outside world didn't exist. Yes, I may have done my job.

Just like any changes in behavior, your engagement with wealth creation may activity directed toward realizing essential life outcomes. In a nutshell, me influencing you balls down to you being motivated from your internal experiences, cognitions, and emotions and will be the direct causes of motivated action that you will take.

All social contexts and external events motivate or trigger your motives expression through behavior, engagement, and self-report. Since you don't exist in a vacuum, however, your experiences cannot take place without some degree of influence, be it in the form of consequences, incentives, or other forms of pressure arising out of the social context of our environment.

The Closing

All needs are born either out of deficiency or need for growth. Physical needs are a particularly strong force in determining behavior. Your body will signal your brain if your wellbeing is threatened, and this can lead to avoidance and procrastination when you are suffering from hunger, thirst, or lack of sleep, for example.

Your vision or needs for wealth creation are born of your desire to change a situation. When you are no longer able to change a situation, you are challenged to change yourselves. If you have little or no need for achievement, you may experience negative affect, such as anxiety, shame, and embarrassment while engaging in that challenging task and will avoid or procrastinate as a result.

Your thoughts can also influence your tendency to avoid or procrastinate. Thoughts are mental constructs like goals, mindset, expectations, beliefs, and self-concept, to name a few that influence your motivation. If you have conflicting goals, for example, you may be more likely to avoid or procrastinate. Change the way you look at things and the things you look at change.

We may feel joy or pride at the possibility of goal attainment through engagement in a particular behavior, or we can be afraid of failure and choose to avoid or procrastinate. Our environment can also be either ideal and supportive or an obstacle to staying motivated and achieving our goals

Understand, that our relationships can be supportive and empowering when it comes to change. Often explained where your relationships support your potential. They can also be demotivating as in where the relationship brings out the worst in you and can contribute to procrastination and avoidance.

Always being aware of how motivation varies over time is particularly important when it comes to goal setting. Short-term goals work better for uninteresting activities as they boost commitment by providing feedback on progress more often, which further reinforces the effort to persist.

Motivation to perform routine or boring activities can be improved; however, by providing clarity of goals and choice in how to perform a task. Clarity and choice can fuel a sense of mastery and autonomy, and both, in combination, can increase overall motivation as they satisfy basic psychological needs.

When it comes to interesting tasks, long-term goals work better as they often provide for greater flexibility and more autonomy in how to pursue them. Short terms milestones can feel intrusive for interesting activities. You are often motivated to perform them because they produce enjoyment. But most importantly, we are motivated to pursue them in the absence of external rewards or incentives.

We also need to keep in mind that motivation to act on the goals is often higher when the goal is sooner rather than later, while far-off goals do not create the tension of immediacy that would motivate us to act right away

When it comes to influencers as I started with this book each chapter was designed to cause an effect on you. Did I motivate you? Everyone experiences changes in their motivation.

Sometimes you might feel fired up and highly driven to reach your goals, while at other times you might feel listless or unsure of what you want or how to achieve it.

Even if you're feeling low on motivation, consider some steps you can take that will keep you moving forward. Some things you can do include:

Adjust your goals to focus on things that matter to you

If you're tackling something that is just too big, break it up into smaller steps and try setting your sights on the first step toward progress

Improve your confidence

Remind yourself about what you achieved in the past and where your strengths lie

If there are things you feel insecure about, try working on making improvements in those areas so that you feel more skilled and capable.

As you seek to be motivated or influenced, maybe it is wealth creation, it could be generational wealth or simply leaving a legacy. It all is going to require you to be motivated, influenced, and change of mindset but most importantly is that you remain consistent in every single thing that you have learned through this book.

You are aware that maintaining consistency is an essential thing but all of us, at some point or the other, struggle to be consistent in what we do. Or in other words, even though the concept of staying consistent seems very simple on the surface, most people struggle with this idea.

They find it difficult to stay consistent because there are just too many distractions. People are simply not focused, committed, or disciplined enough to stick with something in the short-term for long-term results. Wealth creation is a good idea is it not?

Today, you look for instant gratification and in the want of that, you fail to acknowledge that some things do take time. (Wealth Creation) When you don't get immediate results, you don't see the point in continuing those actions over the long run. But consistency isn't about obtaining quick results, rather it's about maintaining incremental progress over some time.

I recently spoke with a pastor and we were talking about this very issue. Three words stayed with me as I left his presence thinking about how I can relay this to you each of you. Here it goes!

Patience is the key to consistency. You have to be patient and focus your efforts diligently in one direction to produce quality, lasting, tangible results. One of the main reasons people don't stick with what they're doing, whatever it might be, is simply impatience. A good example of this is in the world of diet. People try something for a week or two and, impatient for results, immediately run off to the next interesting thing that they see in an ad or on a website.

Your belief likewise, failing to believe in what you're doing will kill your consistency in doing it. Or, to look at it another way, make you much more consistent at NOT doing it. Your consistency, or lack thereof, in what you do is a good indication of your true belief about it.

Your perceived value for a particular thing, which results from the action you need to take should be taken into consideration. Everything that we do is generally motivated by one of two things: fear and desire.

In either case, you take action based on perceived value: running from a bear has the value of saving your life while running as a form of running has the value of maintaining your health. It is a natural tendency that if you fail to see some kind of return from whatever you're doing, you are automatically demotivated and as a result, your consistency suffers

Okay, do not get overconfident there are always potential pitfalls, here are a few things you should watch for that might hurt your efforts:

Quick fixes or all-or-nothing thinking. It's easy to feel unmotivated if you can't fix something immediately. Remind yourself that reaching your goals takes time.

Thinking that one size fits all. Just because an approach or method worked for someone else does not mean that it will work for you. If something isn't helping you reach your goals or is making you feel unmotivated, look for things that will work better for you.

Be sure to follow me on all social media.

WWW.IAMROBWILSON.COM

MAKE SURE THAT YOU ARE READING EACH BOOK OF THE SERIES

Made in United States
North Haven, CT
10 November 2026

22095614R00063